DEC   2005

CHEETAHS

A TRUE BOOK®

by
Ann O. Squire

Children's Press®

A Division of Scholastic Inc.

New York Toronto London Auckland Sydney
Mexico City New Delhi Hong Kong
Danbury, Connecticut

Cheetah cubs

Reading Consultant
Nanci R. Vargus, Ed.D.
Assistant Professor,
School of Education,
University of Indianapolis

Content Consultant
Kathy Carlstead, Ph.D.
Research Scientist,
Honolulu Zoo

Dedication:
For Evan

Library of Congress Cataloging-in-Publication Data

Squire, Ann.
   Cheetahs / Ann O. Squire.
      p. cm. — (True books)
Summary: Describes the physical characteristics, habitats, and behavior of cheetahs.
   ISBN 0-516-22792-0 (lib. bdg.)   0-516-27932-7 (pbk.)
   1. Cheetah—Juvenile literature. [1. Cheetah.] I. Title. II. True book.
QL737.C23S639 2003
599.759—dc21

                                                 2003005174

CHILDREN'S PRESS, and A TRUE BOOK™, and associated logos are trademarks and or registered trademarks of Scholastic Library Publishing. SCHOLASTIC and associated logos are trademarks and or registered trademarks of Scholastic Inc.

1 2 3 4 5 6 7 8 9 10 R 14 13 12 11 10 09 08 07 06 05

Contents

A cheetah running at top speed

Meet a Cheetah

Imagine that you are riding in your family's car, whizzing down the highway at 60 miles (97 kilometers) per hour. Suddenly, something outside catches your eye. You watch in amazement as a beautiful spotted cat races past, leaving your car in the dust. What kind of animal could possibly outrun a car? There's only one: the cheetah. The world's fastest land animal, a cheetah can reach a top speed of 70 miles (113 km) per hour.

Though it's fun to imagine, the scene above could never really happen, because there are no cheetahs in North America. In fact, there are only about twelve thousand wild cheetahs left in the world. They live on the **savannas**, or grasslands, of southern and eastern Africa.

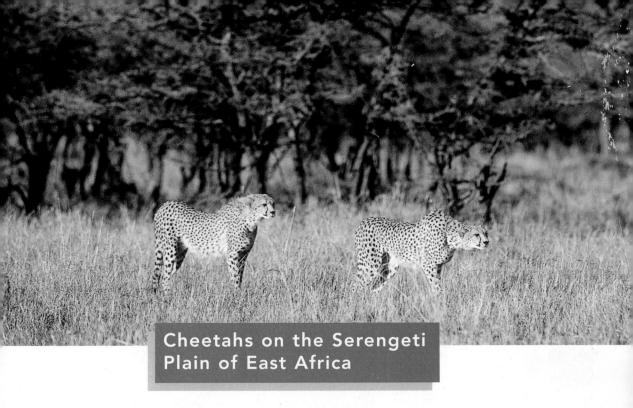

Cheetahs on the Serengeti Plain of East Africa

Cheetahs are smaller than most other big cats, weighing only about 100 to 130 pounds (45 to 59 kilograms). They have slender bodies, long legs, and small heads with rounded ears. Their **tawny** coats are

The cheetah's slim body and long legs help make it a superb runner.

covered with black spots that help them to blend in with their grassland environment.

One sure way to recognize a cheetah is by the long, black stripes that run from the inside corner of each eye down to the mouth. These stripes are called "tear lines." Scientists believe that the dark tear lines help protect the cheetah's eyes from the glaring African sun.

This photograph shows the black "tear lines" on a cheetah's face.

The Cat with No Roar

Did
you know
that cheetahs are
the only big cats that cannot roar? Instead, they
use chirping and purring sounds to communicate
and show their feelings. Cheetahs usually purr
the loudest when they are grooming or sitting
next to each other.

Built for Speed

Like other big cats, cheetahs hunt other animals for food. But while lions and leopards hunt at night, cheetahs **pursue** their **prey** during the daytime. This makes it much more difficult for cheetahs to sneak up on swift-footed gazelles, springboks, and impalas. The

A cheetah looks for prey while hiding behind tall grasses.

cheetah's spotted coat helps it hide in the tall grass, but to capture a prey animal, this cat needs more than **camouflage**. Fortunately, cheetahs are champion runners, and their sleek, lightweight bodies are built for speed.

   With its long, powerful legs, a cheetah can cover up to 20 feet (6 meters) in one stride. Its backbone is very flexible, working almost like a giant spring to push the cheetah

A cheetah's body is designed for speed.

along. The cheetah's heart and lungs are extra large to help give this cat the oxygen it needs for fast sprints. A long tail helps the cheetah keep its balance as it runs.

Even the cheetah's feet are designed to help it run. Unlike other cats, the cheetah has claws that do not **retract**. This means that they cannot be pulled back into the paw. In fact, because of its doglike paws, some people used to think that cheetahs were part cat and part dog!

The claws of a cheetah do not retract.

Since they are always pushed out, the cheetah's claws become blunt and very strong. They help the cheetah grip the ground during quick turns. They also help the animal push off, just as

A cheetah makes a quick turn while chasing a bush hare.

rubber-soled track shoes help runners to get a fast start. A cheetah can accelerate, or gain speed, faster than most cars, going from 0 to 70 miles (113 km) per hour in just a few seconds.

You would think that a cat as fast as the cheetah would be able to outrun just about any prey animal. Surprisingly, though, a cheetah's chase is often unsuccessful. This is because the cheetah can sprint for only a minute or so before it becomes too tired to continue.

Cheetahs can run incredibly fast, but they tire quickly. Here a cheetah is shown yawning while resting after a hunt.

Cheetahs in History

People have been fascinated by cheetahs for thousands of years. As early as 3000 B.C., people used cheetahs to help them hunt. Akbar the Great, an Indian emperor who lived around A.D. 1550, kept several thousand cheetahs. He used them in a sport called coursing. A blindfolded cheetah would be brought within range of a gazelle. The blindfold was removed, and the audience cheered as the cheetah brought down its prey.

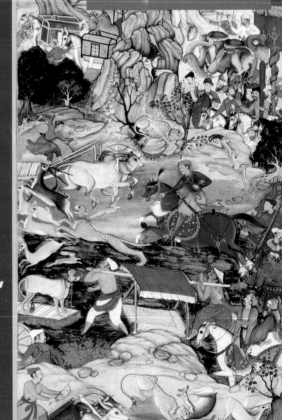

A historical painting showing Akbar the Great using cheetahs to help him hunt gazelle

What's for Dinner?

Cheetahs spend a lot of time looking for something to eat. They hunt mainly in the morning and early evening. The middle of the day is usually quite hot on the savanna, so cheetahs usually rest during that time.

If you visit Africa, you might spot a cheetah perched on top

19

Cheetahs standing on a termite mound, searching the savanna for prey

of a small hill or termite mound, scanning the savanna for prey. The cheetah's sharp eyesight allows it to spot a prey animal as far away as 3 miles (5 km). Cheetahs usually hunt medium- or small-sized animals, such as

gazelles, impalas, and even rab-
bits and birds. They are always
on the lookout for young or
injured animals that may not be
able to get away easily.

Once a cheetah has spotted
its victim, it creeps toward it
through the tall grass. When it

A cheetah getting
ready to attack

is within a few hundred feet, the cheetah springs forward. Its body is a blur as it races toward the prey. By the time the animal notices the cheetah, it is usually too late to escape. As the cheetah closes in on its victim, it reaches out with a front paw. The cheetah uses a sharp claw on the inside of its front leg called a dewclaw to hook the frightened animal and trip it. Then the cheetah bites down on the

These young cheetahs are about to bring down an impala.

animal's throat, cutting off its air supply. Within a few seconds, the captured animal stops breathing and dies.

After it has captured its prey, the cheetah is often too exhausted to eat right away. It drags the prey to a hidden

A cheetah dragging a freshly killed
Thomson's gazelle to a safe place (top) and
a family of cheetahs feasting on a kill (bottom)

spot and then lies down to catch its breath. Once the cheetah has rested for 20 or 30 minutes, it begins to eat as fast as it can. There is always a danger that lions, vultures, or hyenas will try to steal its food. With its light-weight body and blunt claws, the cheetah cannot defend itself very well. So when a larger, more **aggressive** animal comes by, the cheetah backs off. The prey it has captured becomes a meal for another animal.

Cheetah Cubs

Most cat species are solitary, meaning that they live by themselves. Scientists used to think that cheetahs were solitary as well. Now they know that this isn't always true. Male cheetahs often live with two or three other males (usually their brothers), and females are

A group of cheetahs resting under the shade of a tree

sometimes found with other females or cubs. The only time that male and female cheetahs get together, however, is for mating. After mating, the male cheetah leaves.

In about three months, the female gives birth to a litter of blind, helpless cubs. The mother cheetah hides her cubs carefully. She also moves them frequently, sometimes taking them to a new hiding place every few days.

At first the cubs drink only mother's milk. Later, they begin eating meat that the mother brings back for them.

A mother cheetah nursing her newborn cubs

The mother cheetah has a hard job finding enough food for herself and her cubs. After a few weeks, they begin to follow her, hiding in the tall grass as she hunts.

At this age, the cubs look very different from adult cheetahs. Instead of a sleek, spotted coat, a baby cheetah has long grayish hair that forms a ridge on its head, neck, and back. It looks almost like a Mohawk haircut! Some scientists think that this

Young cheetah cubs have a Mohawk-like ridge of fur along their backs.

ridge makes the cub look bigger, so **predators** may be less likely to attack it. It may also make the cub look a bit like a honey badger, one of the fiercest animals on the savanna. In addition, the cub's

Some experts think that a cheetah cub's fur (above) helps fool other animals into thinking that the cub is the fierce honey badger (right).

coat serves as camouflage, helping the cub blend in with its surroundings.

When the cubs are between two and three months old, the long ridge hairs begin to fall out. Soon they are replaced by the spotted adult coat.

As the cubs grow older, their mother teaches them how to hunt. First they watch her as she captures a prey animal. Later, she starts to bring back animals that are still alive, so the cubs can learn how to make the killing bite.

After about eighteen months, the cubs have learned how to

As part of teaching her cubs to hunt, a mother cheetah may catch an animal, release it, and let the cubs finish the kill.

hunt and survive on their own. The mother leaves to mate and raise a new litter. The female cubs also go their separate ways. The male cubs may go off by themselves or they may remain together for life.

Cheetahs in Danger

The cheetah is one of the most rarely seen animals on the African plains. In years to come, as the cheetah population drops even further, cheetahs will be even harder to spot.

Cheetahs in the wild face many threats. Lions and

A lion chasing a cheetah

hyenas not only steal their food but often kill and eat cheetah cubs. Scientists estimate that two out of every three cheetah cubs die before they are two years old. Cheetahs also have a shorter lifespan than other cats. They live only about seven to ten years in the wild, so they are not able to have enough cubs during their lifetime to keep the population going.

Another big threat is loss of the cheetah's **habitat**. As the human population grows, the wide-open spaces that cheetahs need for hunting are being turned into farms

As humans take over more and more land in Africa, there are fewer places where cheetahs can live.

and ranches. Gazelles and impalas are forced out and hungry cheetahs turn to cattle and other livestock for food.

This angers the ranchers, who kill cheetahs whenever they see them.

Poachers are also threatening the cheetah. Poachers are people who hunt animals illegally. Even though it is against the law, poachers kill cheetahs for their beautiful spotted fur, which is used to make coats, rugs, and other objects.

There's no doubt that cheetahs are close to **extinction**.

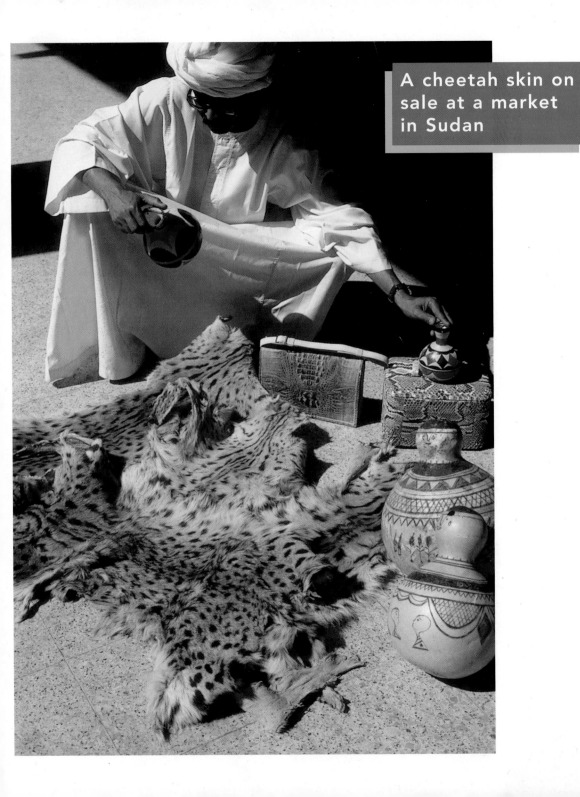

A cheetah skin on sale at a market in Sudan

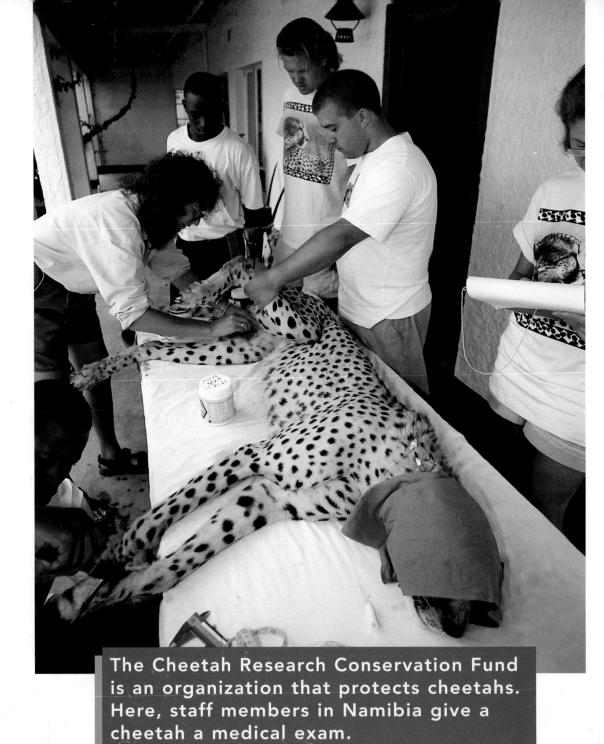

The Cheetah Research Conservation Fund is an organization that protects cheetahs. Here, staff members in Namibia give a cheetah a medical exam.

People are working hard to save them, however. Many areas of Africa have been set aside as parks and reserves in order to protect cheetahs from hunters and angry ranchers. Some ranchers are using electric fences and other methods to keep cheetahs away rather than kill them. A few ranchers have even turned their ranches into wildlife parks. This lets them make money from tourists and still protect cheetahs.

Cheetahs and many other native African animals are protected at such places as the Masai Mara National Reserve in Kenya.

Another way to save an endangered species is to breed the animals in zoos. Unfortunately, this has been difficult with cheetahs. Wildlife **biologists** are continuing to look for ways to breed more **captive** cheetahs. The hope is that then these magnificent cats may someday be returned to the wild.

To Find Out More

Here are some additional resources to help you learn more about cheetahs:

 **Books**

Claybourne, Anna. **Cheetah: Habitats, Life Cycles, Food Chains, Threats.** Raintree, 2003.

Denis-Huot, Christine. **The Cheetah: Fast As Lightning.** Charlesbridge Publishing, 2004.

Esbensen, Barbara Juster. **Swift as the Wind: The Cheetah.** Orchard Books, 1996.

Stille, Darlene R. **Cheetahs.** Compass Point Books, 2003.

Organizations and Online Sites

Cheetah Conservation Fund

http://www.cheetah.org/

This is the Web site of the Namibia-based Cheetah Conservation Fund. This site has lots of information on cheetahs and their conservation, plus a special page for kids.

The Cheetah Spot

http://www.cheetahspot. com/

This site includes all kinds of information about cheetahs.

Cheetahs in a Hot Spot

http://www.pbs.org/wnet/ nature/cheetahs/

This is the Web site companion to a PBS program entitled "Cheetahs in a Hot Spot." It includes lots of cheetah information and links to other cheetah sites.

Important Words

aggressive fierce, threatening

biologists people who study living things

camouflage coloring that helps animals blend in with their surroundings

captive describing an animal that has been taken out of its habitat and is being cared for by humans

extinction when a type, or species, of living thing dies out

habitat place where a living thing naturally lives and grows

predators animals that eat other animals

prey animal eaten by other animals

pursue go after; chase

retract to pull back

savannas grassy plains with few trees

tawny having a light, sandy-brown color

Index

Meet the Author

Ann O. Squire has a Ph.D. in animal behavior. Before becoming a writer, she spent several years studying African electric fish and the special signals they use to communicate with each other. Dr. Squire is the author of many books on animals and natural-science topics, including *Lions, Tigers, African Animals,* and *Animal Babies*. She and her children, Emma and Evan, share their home with a not-so-wild cat named Isabel.